# KILLER
# SNAKES

CLASH

CLASH

by ticktock

Copyright © ticktock Entertainment Ltd 2008

First published in Great Britain in 2008 by ticktock Media Ltd,
2 Orchard Business Centre, North Farm Road, Tunbridge Wells, Kent, TN2 3XF

*project editor: Ruth Owen*
*ticktock project designer: Sara Greasley*
*ticktock picture researcher: Lizzie Knowles*

**With thanks to series editors Honor Head and Jean Coppendale, and consultant Sally Morgan**

**Thank you to Lorraine Petersen and the members of nasen**

ISBN 978 1 84696 744 3 pbk

Printed in China

A CIP catalogue record for this book is available from the British Library.

Picture credits (t=top; b=bottom; c=centre; l=left; r=right):
age fotostock / SuperStock: 10. Bruce Davidson/ naturepl.com: 12. FLPA/FLPA: 16-17. Michael & Patricia Fogden/
Minden Pictures/ FLPA: 7, 21t, 21b, 29. Jeff Greenberg/ Alamy: 28. How Hwee Young/ epa/ Corbis: 11. Claus Meyer/
Minden Pictures/ FLPA: 6. NHPA/Daniel Heuclin: 4, 24. NHPA/ Bill Love: 15.
Tony Phelps/ naturepl.com: 29b. Photolibrary Group: 26. Michael Richards/ John Downer/ naturepl.com: 8.
Jeffrey L. Rotman/CORBIS: 25. Shutterstock: OFC, 1, 2, 5, 9, 14, 18, 19 all, 20, 22-23, 31. Rungroj Yongrit/ epa/
Corbis: 13.

Every effort has been made to trace copyright holders, and we apologise in advance for any omissions. We would be
pleased to insert the appropriate acknowledgments in any subsequent edition of this publication.

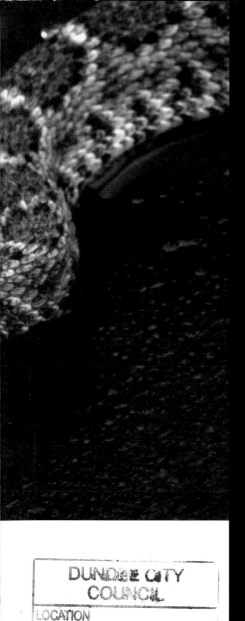

# CONTENTS

# KILLER SNAKES

**Every year 100,000 people die from snake bites! Most victims live in the countryside of Africa, India and south-east Asia.**

Indian cobra

People die because they cannot get to a hospital for treatment. The venom in the snake bite attacks their body before they can get help.

**Cape cobra**

The Cape cobra is one of Africa's most dangerous snakes. The venom in a single bite can kill a person in just a few hours.

Fang

Drop of venom

# Snake venom is very poisonous saliva.

# FANGS

**Snakes bite their prey with two long, pointed teeth called fangs.**

Venom is squirted through the fangs.

Hog-nosed pit viper

Fangs

Frog

# VENOM

There are two main types of snake venom.

## Neurotoxin

**How it works:** it stops your nerves working so they cannot carry messages to your muscles.
**What happens:** you cannot breathe. You die within hours if you don't get treatment.
**Snakes with this venom:** cobras, mambas.

Spitting cobra

Spitting cobras spit their venom into their prey's eyes. They can hit their target from 3 metres away!

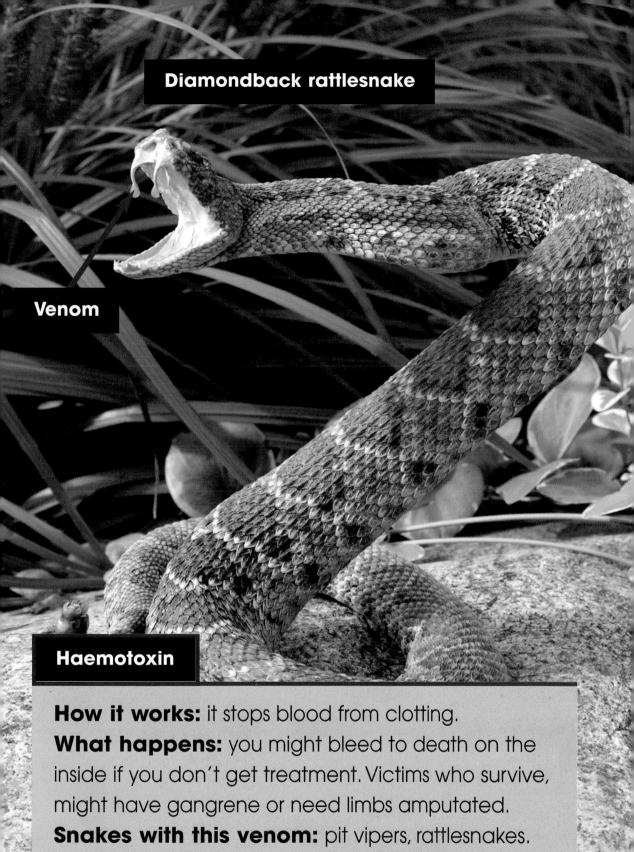

**Diamondback rattlesnake**

**Venom**

**Haemotoxin**

**How it works:** it stops blood from clotting.
**What happens:** you might bleed to death on the
inside if you don't get treatment. Victims who survive,
might have gangrene or need limbs amputated.
**Snakes with this venom:** pit vipers, rattlesnakes.

# TOP KILLERS

**The snakes that kill the most people are the**

- Krait (Asia)
- Indian cobra (Asia)
- Black mamba (Africa)
- Puff adder (Africa)

Snakes are normally scared of people. They only bite if they are disturbed and feel they are in danger.

**Krait**

The krait's venom is the most powerful of the top four killer snakes. Kraits are active at night and they rest in the day.

The most venomous snake in the world is the fierce snake, or inland taipan. It comes from Australia.

The venom in a single bite could kill 100 people!

**Fierce snake**

Here, animal expert Steve Irwin holds a fierce snake.

Irwin studied and cared for wild animals at his zoo in Australia. He often worked with dangerous animals, such as snakes and crocodiles. Irwin was killed by a stingray in 2006.

When there is a threat, a king cobra will rise up to attack. Its head can be 1.5 metres above the ground.

# KING COBRA

**The king cobra is the longest venomous snake in the world. It can grow to over 5 metres long.**

This man is Khum Chaibuddee. In 2006, he set a world record for snake kissing. He kissed 19 king cobras!

In 1999, a Malaysian zookeeper called Mahaguru Sani also set a record. He spent 35 days locked in a room with 250 cobras.

**Just one bite from a cobra and the men might have been killed!**

# BLACK MAMBA

**Half of the people bitten by black mambas die. Even baby mambas have a deadly bite!**

Mambas normally stay hidden from people. However, in 2006 there was a heatwave in South Africa. Because it was so hot, more baby mambas hatched from their eggs than normal.

Hundreds of baby mambas invaded the city of Durban. They were all looking for a place to live.

The city's snake catchers were kept busy catching the baby mambas.

Thankfully no one was bitten!

Black mambas are fast.
They can slither faster
than a person can run.

# DEADLY SQUEEZE

Pythons and constrictors squeeze their prey to death.

They wrap their huge bodies tight around their victims.

Crocodile

Every time the victim breathes out,
the snake tightens its grip.

The prey suffocates to death.

Rock python

# SWALLOW HARD

**Snakes do not chew their food. They swallow it whole!**

First, the snake kills its prey using its venom or by squeezing its victim to death.

Corn snake

Mouse

Lower jaw

Then the snake slithers its own body over its meal until everything is inside.

Sometimes the snake's prey isn't completely dead.

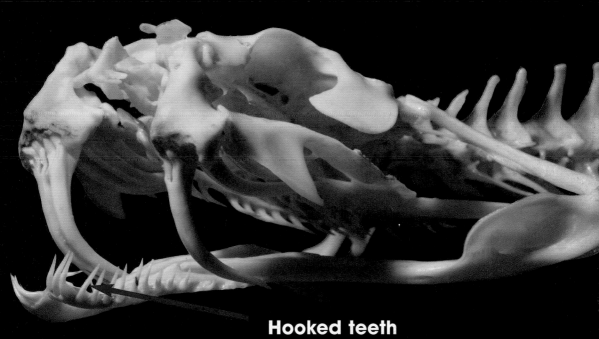

**Hooked teeth**

Then the snake uses its hooked teeth to hold the struggling prey as it is...

## ...swallowed alive!

# WARNING!

A snake's venom is its main way of catching prey and defending itself. So, it doesn't want to waste it.

Most venomous snakes give a warning before they attack.

**Rattlesnake**

**Rattle**

If you corner a rattlesnake, it will use the rattle on its tail to frighten you off. The rattle is made of dead skin. It grows longer as the snake gets older.

Venomous coral snakes have bright warning stripes.
But some non-venomous snakes have copied this.

**Coral snake**

A coral snake has red stripes touching yellow stripes.

**Kingsnake**

A kingsnake is non-venomous. Its red stripes
touch black stripes.

**Remember this old rhyme:**
**Red touch yellow, kill a fellow.**
**Red touch black, venom lack.**

# SURVIVE A SNAKE BITE

## Been bitten?

- Don't panic! Non-venomous snakes bite, too. Even the dangerous ones do not always use their venom.

- Keep still. Moving will pump the venom around your body.

- Let the bite bleed. Then wash and bandage it.

- If possible, hold the bite at the same height as your heart. This will help to stop the venom spreading through your body.

- Remember what the snake looks like. Then you can describe it to a doctor.

## Get to a hospital fast!

# SNAKE BITE CURES

**Snake bites are treated with medicines called antivenins.**

Antivenins are actually made from snake venom!

Snake venom is valuable stuff. A kilogram of dried venom is worth half a million pounds.

**Indian cobra**

The man in this photo is trying to catch an Indian cobra. The man makes a living catching snakes. He catches them so their venom can be collected.

Collecting the venom is known as milking the snake.

**Venom**

The venom is then injected into a large animal, such as a horse. The horse's blood makes chemicals to fight the venom. The venom doesn't hurt the horse.

The horse's blood is then used to make the antivenin.

# SNAKE MUM

Snakes may be deadly killers, but many are caring mums.

Egg

A female python wraps her body around
her eggs.

She shivers her muscles to make heat.
This keeps the eggs warm until they hatch.

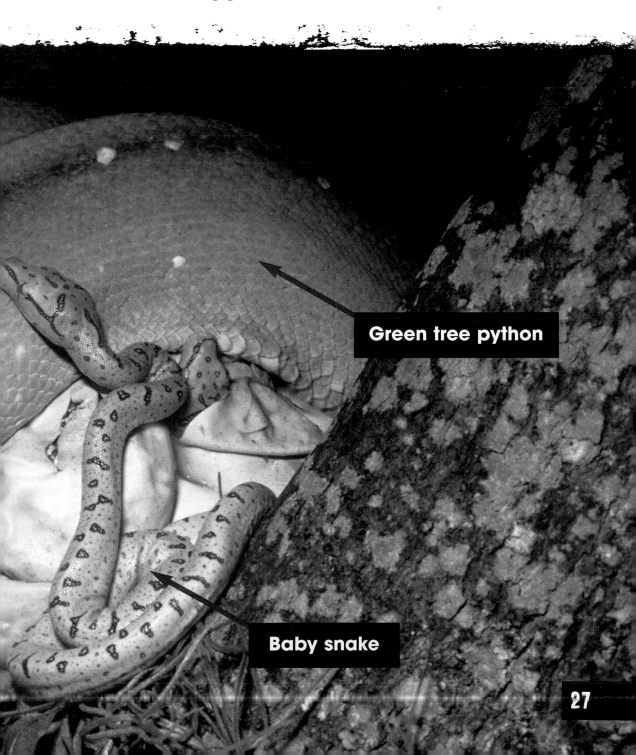

Green tree python

Baby snake

# SOS – SAVE OUR SNAKES

**Many species of snake are endangered. They need help!**

People often kill venomous snakes because they are afraid of them. Snakes lose their habitat when people clear land to build homes or grow crops.

Zoo visitors hold a python.

There is some good news. Zoos give snakes a safe place to live. They also teach visitors about the snakes.

Many zoos are breeding endangered snakes. Sometimes zoo-bred snakes can go back to the wild.

The Australian woma python is very endangered.

**Woma python**

In September 2007, nine zoo-bred womas were put back into the wild in a safe nature reserve.

There are fewer than 250 Aruba rattlesnakes left.

**Aruba rattlesnake**

Zoos around the world are taking part in about 35 Aruba breeding programmes.

# NEED TO KNOW WORDS

**amputate** To remove a body part, such as a hand or leg.

**breeding** Putting male and female animals together so they mate and have young.

**captivity** Living in a cage or enclosure, such as in a zoo, on a farm or as a pet.

**clotting** When liquid blood becomes jelly-like and doesn't flow any more.

**defend** To protect.

**endangered** At risk of dying out so there are no more of that animal species left.

**fang** A long, sharp tooth. Snake fangs are hollow so venom can be pumped through them.

**gangrene** A very bad infection. Sometimes a body part has to be removed if it has gangrene.

**habitat** The place where an animal lives. Snakes live in many different habitats, from forests to deserts.

**hatch** To break out of an egg.

**prey** An animal that is hunted by another animal as food.

**saliva** Liquid (spit) produced in the mouth.

**species** A group of animals that look similar and can breed with each other.

**suffocate** When an animal or person dies because they cannot breathe.

**venom** Poisonous saliva.

**venomous** A snake that produces and uses venom to kill prey and to defend itself.

**victim** A person or animal who is hurt or killed.

# SNAKES AS PETS

## Would you like a pet snake? Think it through carefully...

*Corn snakes make good pets. They grow up to 1.5 metres long.*

- Many snakes can live for over 20 years. Do you want to live with your snake for that long?

- Keeping a python might seem like fun, but it could grow to over 3 metres long!
  Do you have enough room?

- Always choose a snake born in captivity. Wild snakes should not be caught and kept as pets.

- Get some expert advice:
  *http://www.scales-tails.co.uk/careguides.php*

# SNAKES ONLINE

## Websites

*http://www.oplin.org/snake/*

*http://nationalzoo.si.edu/Animals/ReptilesAmphibians/Exhibit/default.cfm*

*http://www.nationalgeographic.com/kingcobra/index-n.html*

# INDEX